P9-DYD-745

E
DOW

Downing, Johnette.

Today is Monday in
Louisiana.

$15.95

DATE			

BAKER & TAYLOR

Today Is Monday in Louisiana

By Johnette Downing
Illustrated by Deborah Ousley Kadair

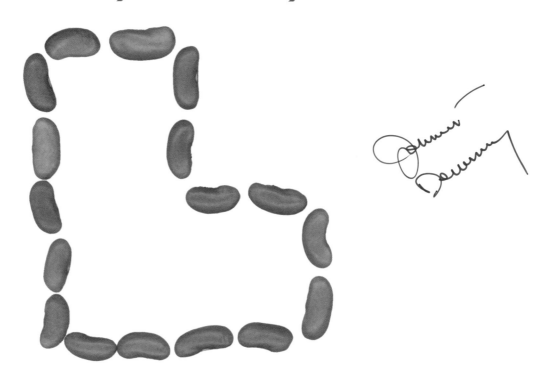

PELICAN PUBLISHING COMPANY
Gretna 2006

*The word "Pelican" and the depiction of a pelican are
trademarks of Pelican Publishing Company, Inc., and
are registered in the U.S. Patent and Trademark Office.*

Library of Congress Cataloging-in-Publication Data

Downing, Johnette.
  Today is Monday in Louisiana / by Johnette Downing ; illustrated by
Deborah Ousley Kadair.
       p. cm.
  Summary: Illustrations and rhythmic text celebrate edible treats that
characterize Louisiana, such as beignets and po' boys. Includes facts about
the foods mentioned and a recipe for red beans and rice.
  ISBN-13: 978-1-58980-406-7 (hardcover : alk. paper)
  [1. Food habits—Fiction. 2. Cookery, Cajun—Fiction. 3. Louisiana—
Fiction.] I. Kadair, Deborah Ousley, ill. II. Title.
  PZ7.D759277Tod 2006
  [E]—dc22
                                                    2006004223

Printed in Singapore
Published by Pelican Publishing Company, Inc.
1000 Burmaster Street, Gretna, Louisiana 70053

Come and get it!

Today is Monday.

Today is Monday. Monday red beans.

All you lucky children, come and eat it up. Come and eat it up!

Today is Tuesday.

Today is Tuesday. Tuesday po' boys,
Monday red beans.

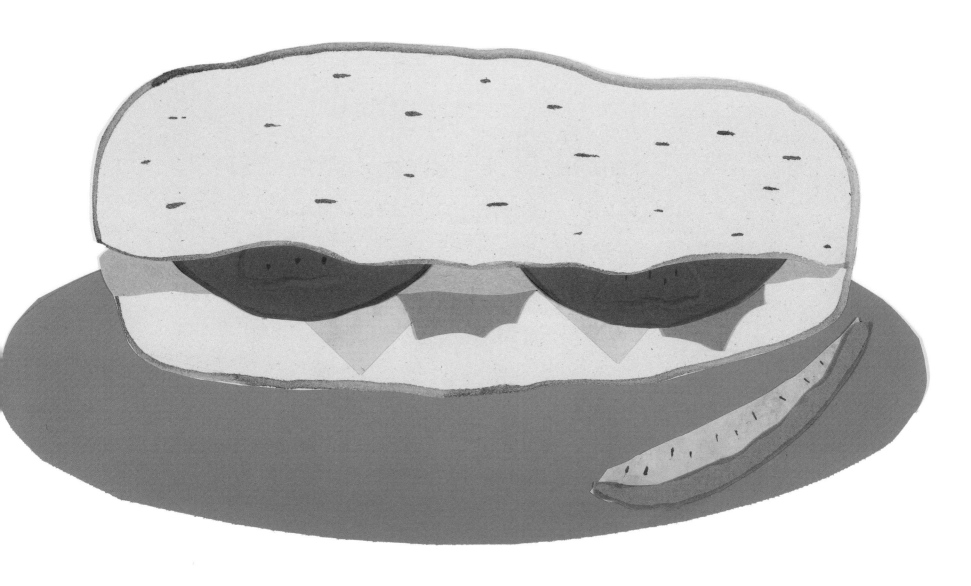

All you lucky children, come and eat it up. Come and eat it up!

Today is Wednesday.

Today is Wednesday. Wednesday gumbo, Tuesday po' boys, Monday red beans.

All you lucky children, come and eat it up. Come and eat it up!

Today is Thursday.

Today is Thursday. Thursday jambalaya, Wednesday gumbo, Tuesday po' boys, Monday red beans.

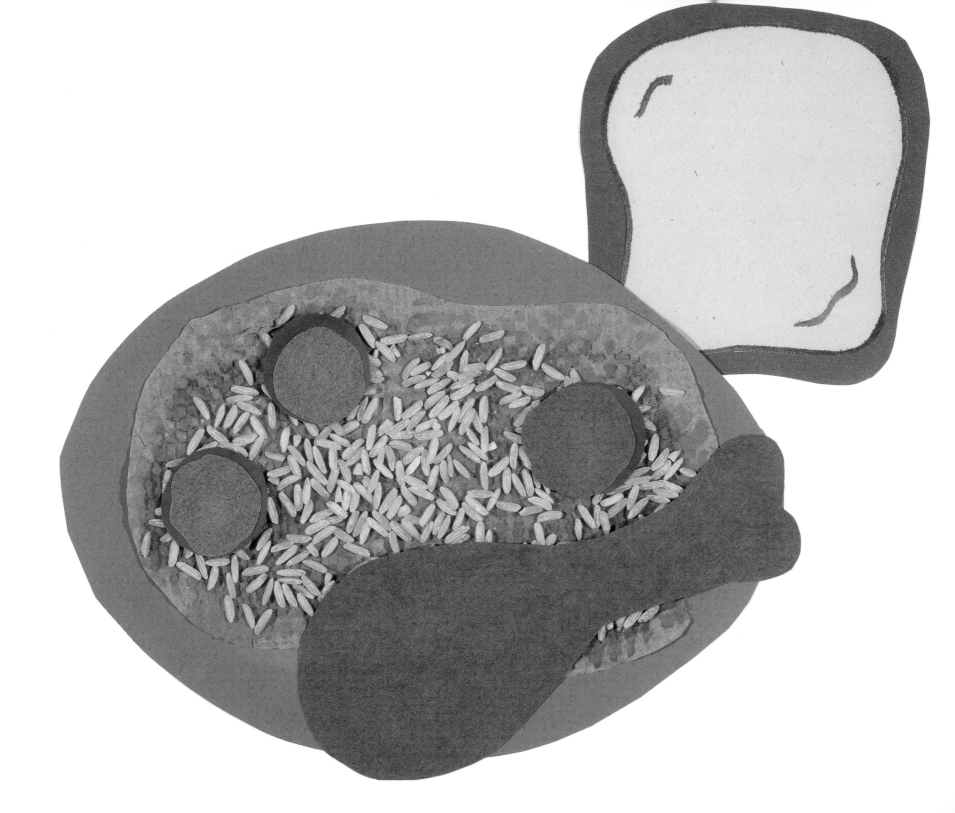

All you lucky children, come and eat it up. Come and eat it up!

Today is Friday.

Today is Friday. Friday catfish, Thursday jambalaya, Wednesday gumbo, Tuesday po' boys, Monday red beans.

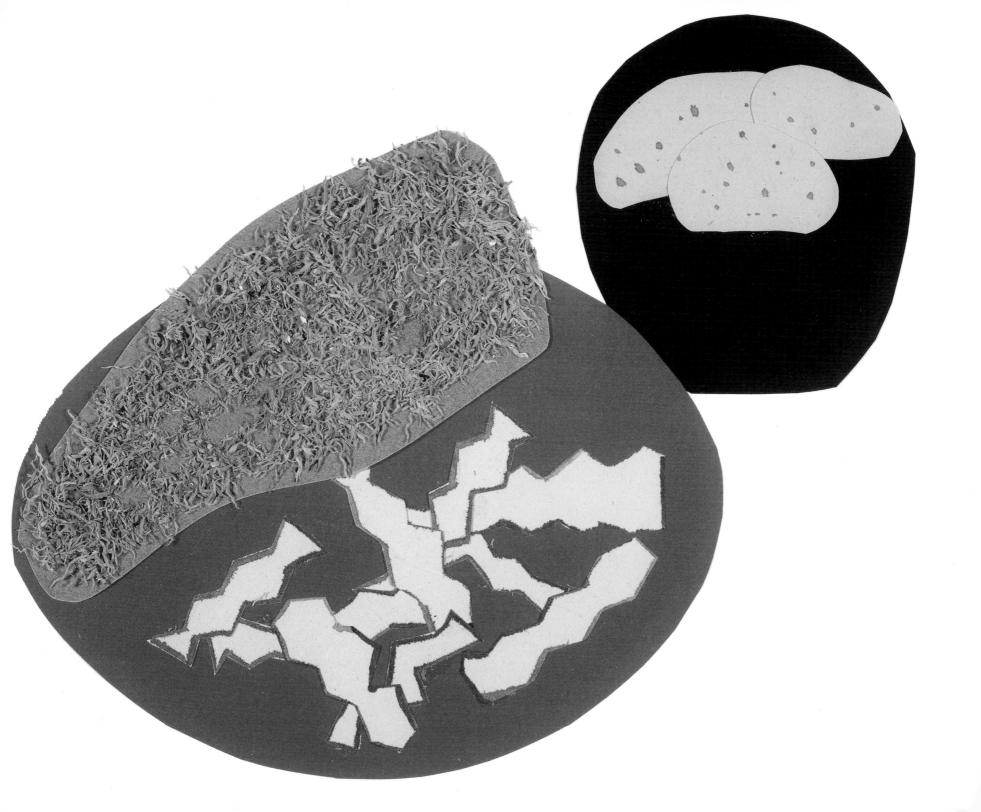

All you lucky children, come and
eat it up. Come and eat it up!

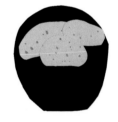

Today is Saturday.

Today is Saturday. Saturday crawfish, Friday catfish, Thursday jambalaya, Wednesday gumbo, Tuesday po' boys, Monday red beans.

All you lucky children, come and eat it up. Come and eat it up!

Today is Sunday.

Today is Sunday. Sunday beignets, Saturday crawfish, Friday catfish, Thursday jambalaya, Wednesday gumbo, Tuesday po' boys, Monday red beans.

All you lucky children, come and eat it up. Come and eat it up! Come and eat it up!

Word Menu

Beignets

A favorite New Orleans breakfast, dessert, or anytime treat. Beignets are rectangular, lightly browned doughnuts with white powdered sugar sprinkled generously on top. They are served warm with a cup of café au lait (coffee with steamed milk) or chocolate milk.

Catfish

A dish typically served in Louisiana on Friday due to a Roman Catholic tradition of not eating meat on that day. Louisiana catfish is usually served fried in a light cornmeal batter.

Crawfish

A crawfish is the Louisiana version of a lobster. Much smaller than the lobster, crawfish are often boiled by the sackful in large pots over an open burner outdoors. Family gatherings and special events are usually celebrated with a crawfish boil. If you ever want company, just mention a crawfish boil and your yard will be filled to the brim with joyful people.

Gumbo

An African word meaning "okra," but most Louisianans will tell you that gumbo starts with a roux, a mixture of oil and flour that gives gumbo its rich brown color. Gumbo is a thick soup with a delicious mix of chicken, sausage, seafood, vegetables, spices, and anything else you may want to add. Filé is a spice made from sassafras leaves that is often sprinkled on the gumbo after it is cooked. Gumbo is served over steamed rice.

Jambalaya

A traditional Louisiana rice dish typically made with sausage, pork, or chicken. Jambalaya is similar to paella from Spain. Creole jambalaya is made with tomatoes, and Cajun jambalaya is made without tomatoes. Like most things in Louisiana, anything goes, which means you are certain to find a little *lagniappe* (something extra) in your jambalaya.

Po' Boys or Poor Boys

A delicious Louisiana sandwich made with French bread. You can order it "dressed," meaning with lettuce, tomato, and mayonnaise, or "plain," which includes just the meat and bread. Po' boys come in delicious varieties such as meatball, roast beef, alligator, crawfish, shrimp, soft shell crab, and almost anything you can imagine.

Red Beans and Rice

A dish typically served in Louisiana on Monday because that day was washday. The meal could be cooked slowly all day without much fuss while the laundry was washed. At the end of the day, the laundry would be clean and the beans would be ready to eat.

Red Beans and Rice

1 lb. dry kidney beans
1 ham bone with ham pieces
2 lb. sausage, sliced
2 stalks celery, chopped
1 large onion, chopped
1 clove garlic, chopped
6 cups water
1 tbsp. Worcestershire sauce
1 bay leaf
Salt, pepper, and parsley to taste
3 cups rice

Soak beans in water overnight. Drain and put aside. Sauté ham pieces, sausage, celery, onion, and garlic. In a large pot, combine all ingredients except rice and bring to a boil. Stir. Reduce heat to low and simmer for several hours until beans are tender. A little water may need to be added until beans are fully cooked. When beans are nearly ready, cook rice. Serve red beans over rice. Feeds four people from Louisiana or six people anywhere else.